LEARN
LOOK

Learning to Look

CHRIS CONSIDINE

PETERLOO POETS

First published in 2003
by Peterloo Poets
The Old Chapel, Sand Lane, Calstock, Cornwall PL18 9QX, U.K.

A catalogue record for this book is available
from the British Library

ISBN   1-904324-05-3

Printed in Great Britain By
Antony Rowe Ltd, Chippenham, Wilts.

ACKNOWLEDGEMENTS

Thanks are due to the editors of the following journals, in which several of the poems in this volume first appeared: *The Interpreter's House, Other Poetry, Poetry Nottingham International* and *Smiths Knoll*.

The sequence *Touched by War* was highly commended in the Blue Nose Poets Competition, 2000.

"Swaledale Millennia", "Seeing Orange", "The Cruellest Class" and "Hole in the Wall" were included in *Swaledale Sketchbook* (Smith/Doorstop Books, 2002). This collection was a winner in The Poetry Business Competition 2002, and short-listed for the Forward Prize in the best first collection category.

south west arts

Contents

TOUCHED BY WAR

STONEWALLERS AND OTHER POEMS

THE LONELYHEARTS COLUMN

LEARNING TO LOOK

TOUCHED BY WAR

1. LOOT

It was a long time
before I met my father
as he lived in another
country called War

which was too far away
for him to travel home
though parcels sometimes came
as evidence of him:

a Mussolini hat
black with golden tassels;
some greyish chocolate
that had melted and reset;

a model cast-iron bath
with legs, enamelled white,
and "Dante Martiri e Figli"
printed along one side;

a bale of blue brocaded
silk for party dresses;
a doll sent with a message
"Call her Anna Maria".

And postcards I still have,
that chart an army's progress
from Catania to Cortina
in shades of grey and sepia,

and on the back of each
"Much love from Daddy" and
three stiff kisses
in a military hand.

2. GRAINS OF SAND

Gill is supported
by her bodyguards
Sally and Nicola.
They drift across the playground
her arms round their waists
their arms round her shoulders.

She cries in lessons.
She is truculent.
She doesn't finish her homework.
She is giving cause for concern.
In the bottom of her pencil box
her precious spoonful of desert.

For her a beach will never again
be innocent. Next summer
she will be too old
for bucket and spade,
too old to bury her father in the sand.
If he comes back.

3. HATE-CHILD

In the black shadow
of the mango tree
she plays with stones
and knotted rags,
giving them names.

Her ten fathers,
for ever marked
with blood from her mother
and her mother's husband,
have rampaged onwards.

Her mother cannot love her
but sometimes when the hands
move on her skin to clothe or wash her
she makes believe their hesitant touch
is a caress.

She knows she must not laugh
or her mother's eyes fearfully
interrogate her face, recalling
others lit with triumph,
other barings of teeth.

Soon she will also know
that when her fathers pressed
on her mother the unwanted
seed of life, they also passed on
to both the seeds of death.

4. STRANGE MEETING

Neither of us was dead, luckily, although
your neatly placed bomb was designed to kill,
our guns swung up to pluck you out of the air.

I'm still not sure what kind of luck mine was –
to see my friends turn into torches;
disfigurements that slide all eyes away.

You had the best of it: the high of triumph,
the hero's welcome. I had the nightmares.
You only had to suffer this meeting,

my face, my hands. "Sorry" one of your few words
of English. What locked us in a tight embrace
was guilt – my friends, your enemies. I named them

to you. Our meeting should have taken place
in gothic vaults or the recollected
fire, smoke, darkness, not in this homely lounge,

with the blue settee, the television set,
your wife's collection of china ornaments,
your ordinary face, dark eyes that didn't see

the ship of souls, only the iron target.
I came to meet the demon of my night
terrors, but you were no more than a man.

5. MR. POD

The neighbours call him Mr. Pod
knowing that is short for something more.
His eyes peer at them from a long way back
in a face all seams and patches.
He speaks little and labours tirelessly
in his garden: a place of order,
trenches and mounds, obedient vegetables.

One evening, there he is
on the six o'clock news, indicted
for the deaths of thousands.
He says he was not that man,
he was elsewhere, remembers nothing.
Cameras catch the sparkle
of light on his wet cheeks,

a shrivelled man whose every cell
is many times changed since then.
With their machines doctors will slice his mind
in search of darknesses. On the first day
of the trial, the next-door neighbours, waking,
are shocked to see each cherished plant
in his garden dead, brown, poisoned.

6. YOUNG MEN

The cadets have not been taken to visit the German
graves – rusty-blood trapdoors into the ground.

These English tombstones are brilliant
white – men were sown and teeth sprang up.

How clean and neat they are, planted with gardens
as if the lost boys' mothers had come here to work off their grief.

As if the innocence of flowers could obliterate
unquiet memories: lice and rats, slime, fear, blood.

The live men walk along the rows
reading the names (or lack of names) and dates.

"He was a year older than me
when he was killed." "This one was my age."

Today they forget to think of girls,
football and beer, or see them far away and haloed.

At the exit they study the cliff
of ordinary names, and many find their own.

7. STREET SCENE

City noise is a comforting background music
heard and not heard, until her ears select
what may be faint backfiring.
Cacophony become more rhythmical,
takes on an edge of panic.
How could the stutter of pneumatic drills
seem to be coming closer?

Mother and child peer through the bamboo blind.
An empty alley. Shouting from the square.
A man steps yawning from the doorway opposite –
jeans, flip-flops, a young smooth torso
whose muscles dance like darker gold
as he pulls on a tee-shirt. When his head
comes through, the black hair bounces back.

A whining slides her eyes right, to seek out
its source. Her son's hands clutch her skin:
Why has Wei-Ping's shirt changed colour?
Why is he sleeping in the dust?

8. THE BRIDGE

This is something I know,
but can't remember.
There were women
bundled up in shawls.

They are stiff with cold and fear
but they must keep moving.
It is vital to cross the bridge
before the soldiers come.

, The water is a whitish green –
can it be the Danube?
Already the edges are stilled
with lace of ice.

And now there is a commotion
behind, just out of sight.
Our hearts jump.
Blood bangs in our ears.

Do it. Now.
Keep faith.
And it is with nothing but love,
my darling,

not pausing to kiss,
to breathe the milky warmth,
on the stone parapet
we, they, I, smash.

You have to be forceful.
A baby's tender skull

is tougher than an eggshell.
So it is done
with vehemence of love.

But is this true?
Who were these women
and what happened to them
when the troops caught up?

9. TANTE ELISE

My black curls
curtained his butter-coloured head
in the meadow.
Brown farmgirl's hand
on the milky skin
of his ribs.

In the hayloft
he glowed gold
in the light that spilled from me.
He kissed my hair.
Our bodies spoke fluently
without the barrier of language.

When they shaved my head
in the marketplace
I was already bereft.
I remember the shock of cold
the hungry eyes
the satiated sigh.

There was no excuse.
I have worn my disgrace
like a headscarf
ever since. Still here
creeping about the yard
despised and useful.

At shearing time
I stay in the kitchen.
I do not want to see
the ewes' humiliation.
My hair is not black now
nor scarlet, but white as theirs.

10. REPRISAL

Because they have only just
cautiously come home
haytime is late this year
but today they will finish.

Ribs of the panting tractors
vibrate. Heat rises from them
transparent as flawed glass
to make horizons fluid.

Last week's meadows
are greening tenderly. Yesterday's
wounded slope is yellow-buff.
This final field, ankle deep

in cut stalks is silvery, bluish,
an inland sea. The old baler
round and round and round
mutters its endless dactyls.

And now men and boys
are heaving the last bales
happy in spite of sweat
grass-dust and flies.

But the birds have stopped singing
to listen: a noisy truck –
gunfire – shouting – a scream –
and when the engine fades

there is perfect silence
under the empty sky
until the women come running,
already sobbing for breath.

STONEWALLERS AND AND OTHER POEMS

Stonewallers

No, not the ones who netted these hills
and stopped them taking off to cruise the sky
like great green whales.

Beach-cricket criticism –
but playing safe made sense to me:
caution, defensiveness, endurance.

And we are a family of stonewallers,
survivors, my parents grimly pleased
to enumerate the funerals of their peers,

my children hanging in there, doggedly
persisting in their chosen courses, beginning
now to produce the next obstinate generation.

Salt of the earth, you might say, people who come
through war, divorce, depression,
the daily dullness of work, (almost) unscathed.

The obituary in the alumni magazine
rekindled envy – her talent, her confident beauty.
Success and worship have made their permanent bright mark.

Bassanio the risk-taker got the prize. Soldiers,
saints, explorers have made the extravagant gesture
and won a kind of immortality.

How satisfying to take a wild swing at the ball
(those fearfully rolled-up and squeezed-together fragments)
and feel the shock of connection,

to snap the restraints of the hills
and see them shiver as the wind pushes them over the edge
to hurtle through the giddy air.

Swaledale Millennia

Midwinter night. Here on this hillside
the shepherd boy listens for wolf, bear,
or fox. The naked trees are singing
to themselves; below him the river
breathes and moves, but the sheep make no noise.
He is ignorant of Roman greed
and dreams, and the sudden excitement
among herdsmen above Bethlehem
as BC ends in stars and music.

Gunnar's cousin, alone with his flock,
knows that the winter solstice is past
and midnight stars hang over the scar,
he has heard the stories of Danish
attacks in the east, of farms on fire,
and of marauding Scots in the north,
but he does not know he should expect
signs and wonders tonight as a new
year breaks with its ominous number.

The old man has cried off the party,
sent his son away. At this distance
there won't be fireworks or jangling bells.
On the opposite slope only two
farms glimmer like candles in blackness.
Sheep silently roam the rough pastures
but there's no money in wool or lambs –
his son may be the last shepherd here.
He waits with a heavy heart among
his magical appurtenances:
heat, light, telephone, multicoloured
square of London life in the corner,
fearing the unimaginable

new millennium. But when he looks
out at midnight, there, still, Orion
emblazons the air over Wensleydale.

Seeing Orange

To my mother this pungent steam
signalled a seasonal chore,
but I, like Marie Antoinette,
am playing countrywoman
and January is marmalade month.

I am a billionaire of time
and silence. Shall I choose, today,
to sing, draw, gaze at the unwearying
beauty of the view? Shall I feel moved
to iron a sheet, paint a wall, scrub a floor?

My fingers are sticky, stiff, swollen with cutting.
It's back to basics, doing it the hard way,
the Zen of preserving – I become one with fruit,
knife, wooden spoon, the heavy pan
her mother gave to mine.

Whispery sugar shifts
in sparkling dunes and dies like snow
into the seething cauldron.
Windows mist and seal me
in sweetness with a bitter edge.

Thick gush into glass.
The molten-metal stream
clots, taking its time, and cools to stasis.
Ranked jars stand glowing
in fluorescent light.

Amber with its suspended life:
fibres of fruit, small-pored

vermilion slivers,
colours of copper, gold,
daffodil, sunrise, fire.

The Cruellest Class

Roofed by drizzling cloud, sheep in their sections
await their turn for judgment.

First the tall sheep: curled Teeswaters,
Bluefaced Leicesters with imperial profiles.

Spotted and spiky Jacobs proud of their lineage,
Dalesbred and Swaledales and thug-faced Texels.

Each breed has its class and peculiar
classicism, its points and pedigree.

But here at the end is a motley group
lumped together as Butchers' Lambs,

some black-headed, some white,
some randomly speckled, slumped,

most of them, on the smirched grass
as if aware of inferiority,

moving their jaws like sullen teenagers.
This one is listlessly nibbling

the blue twine that keeps him penned
fast. Only the smallest one

cries constantly, a bleak complaint
that splits his jaw, shivers the thin grey tongue.

But even these are washed and prinked,
creamy fleeces fluffed up and faces gleaming.

Stars today and meat tomorrow.

Hole in the Wall

On the north side or the south
sheep have sheltered from snow, wind or sun
for more than three hundred years, but now
since the sycamore split in the storm
there is a ten-foot wound. Imagine
the creak and scream of dividing wood,
the crash, the grating rumble of rock.

This downhill spill of stones has laid bare
the wall's history: hammer and axe
marks, surfaces rough as sandpaper
but yellow and young-looking, set with
sparkle-chips like small dewdrops or stars.
This one, petrified sponge and that one
flaky mud-strata. Others are grained

like wood or rippled by ancient seas.
Here is a trove of shells and crinoids
and there a cheese-like wedge darkening
towards the mouldy rind. You can tell
which ones were the outer surfaces:
dirt-speckled or green from looking north,
crusted with grey, white, turquoise, ochre.

Before lambing time Willie and Greg
will come up with landrover, sheepdog
and Radio 2. One on each side
they will tamp the base wide and steady
and taper the rising wall, packed tight
down the centre and knit with throughstones,
towards its coping stone at the top.

Smoking, half-listening and swearing
half-heartedly at the roving dog,
they will sort and select the heavy
irregular slabs packed through with cold
and smelling of old churches. Their hands
though hard and accustomed to the work
will tingle and thrum an hour after.

Female Complaint

After a week of sulks I was glad to see the back of him
I had stopped asking if anything was wrong no point
he was probably hearing voices again Do this Do that
Go to Nineveh anyway he didn't go to Nineveh
because I heard him on the phone to the travel agent
I refrained from suggesting he should go back to work and make
some money instead of squandering it on boat trips
he packed his own suitcase and off he went in a bad temper
because he couldn't find his sunglasses then blissful
peace and quiet for a few days he wouldn't need
sunglasses I thought because the weather was terrible
for July every evening on the weathermap
there seemed to be a new low coming in
over the sea rain gales thunder the lot
served him right swanning off god knows where
the next thing was a phone call at three in the morning
the line was dreadful he'd fallen overboard been shipwrecked
one or the other lost his credit cards could I ring the bank
then it got really garbled he'd been in Wales
or he'd seen a whale he'd been swallowed
and vomited up on a beach I switched off I'm afraid
and let him ramble said Really or Oh dear
or Mmm whenever there was a silence I mean
there had been other episodes I thought of ringing
the doctor but I couldn't find out where Jonah was
he didn't seem to know himself the line went dead
I went back to sleep what was I supposed to do
a week later there was a card from Nineveh
how had he got there I wanted to know
it said glad you are not here so was I
I knew he would turn up eventually and he did
a ring at the front door late one evening he'd lost his keys
but after all that his mood didn't seem to have improved

he slammed the door stamped up the stairs demanded food
I never did get to the bottom of it it's no use asking
I wouldn't get a straight answer and he's still
not back at work though thank goodness he's found
a hobby that gets him out from under my feet
now he spends most of the day in his greenhouse
which is fine as long as his plants are doing all right
life isn't worth living when something fails to thrive
talk about weeping and wailing men are such children
I just switch off and say Yes dear No dear Write to
Gardeners' Question Time I can't be doing with it.

Edith and the Unicorn

My feet remember her snailspace progress
along the Georgian street, with pauses at
presbytery and Conservative Club
to slump against the low wall and railings.
In spite of aching legs and breathlessness
she saw the blue fall of lobelia
from a window box, a wall's 'red ivy'.

Safe in the Oxfam shop she scrutinized
the garment rails with dark myopic eyes,
her grubby fingers stroking the chiffon
and lace, artificial silk and satin.
Regardless of size and reason she chose
her peacock robes: a multicoloured blouse,
a rose-print dress, a sprigged blue petticoat.

Then to the Unicorn for a sit-down
and half of lager, where she would proudly
spread out her purchases until she sat
circled by freshness in the reddish gloom,
and the ancient lady of the legends
was metamorphosed back into beauty,
the sweet-faced virgin in the flowery field.

The House of Honest Despairers

It is hard to come back from the underground country of madness
whose grey air spills after like smoke.
The women who meet in the old gaol
with its thick, small, hardly-opening windows
like the suicide-proof panes of Ward 15
are no longer whole. They have lost their men,
transformed long ago into enemies, their children

time and again to foster-care, their fertility
to powerful medication. They are a quiet group
suspicious-eyed, overweight or dowdy,
out of love with themselves.
Their ornaments are scars – bracelet at wrist,
choker at throat, parallel stripes along arms;
they walk like zombies as if worn down by distance.

This is The Haven, a place without pretence
where you are allowed to sit and do nothing,
admit failure, refuse to eat, lay head on arms, or weep.
This is the house of honest despairers,
each one an Orpheus returning broken from Tartarus
having struggled to the uttermost and still lost.

I imagine them monumental on a bleak hilltop,
a dignity in their stillness to move trees.
The heavy-headed sycamore, the graceful larch,
ash and dark pine glide slowly towards them
and in the shadowy branches overhead
big and small birds gather and sit silent.

William's Silence

I wake to a hangover of shame.
What did I say to my dull virtuous wife
when, like Hermione, she clung
lingeringly to my parting brother's hand?

Today in the church at my park gate
I punish my knees on cold flagstones.
Because my speech has sinned, for seven years
I vow no word shall leave my mouth.

Poor lady, she was always shadowy.
With age she shrinks and stoops. Her voice
is a dry rustle. I answer her with nod
and reverent gesture as if from far off.

Soon she completes her dying, but my penance
is not complete. In the dark church I have forbidden
music and close my ears to the whispering priest.
The Burial of the Dead swims on the page.

Hour after hour I stand by the water
watching my golden carp on their graceful occasions.
I remember the movement of skin on skin
but crave now only a cool slow sliding.

How much more eloquent the minuet
of head, hand, eye than words.
I shrink from the gross chatter
of men and women in their sweaty bustle.

One night I discover thieves. I will not call out
and cannot alert the snoring servants.
I withdraw from the morning's outcry. In the depths
of my ravaged house I myself am inviolate.

No-one speaks and no caged bird sings in my grave rooms.
I am old now and move effortfully across them.
Tomorrow the seven years will be over. Perhaps then
I shall unlock my throat and let the voice go free.

Out of Reach

Whiteness to the horizon, but look!
the northern edge of cloud is hardening
into angles. Those are snow summits over there.

We lose them as we sink among
and even, ghostlike, through
trick mountains, cones of cumulus.

Sometimes in the afternoon through the pollution
we glimpse diminutive peaks
yellow as ancient bone.

At Nagarkot we watch day dawn
as if for the first time ever over Langtangs
tiny and grey as teeth on a serrated blade.

In silence they absorb the rising light,
swell and turn orange, golden,
translucent, points of flame.

Feverish and queasy I sit on the terrace
at Pokhara. The white peaks look down
at me. Dhaulagiri, Annapurna, Hiunchuli,

the holy mountain Machhapuchhre,
disconnected from earth hover above
the foothills at breakfast and sunset.

And then we turned back south. I could have made
a last dash for Everest but it was expensive
and clarity could not be guaranteed. Was I afraid

of the unbreathable air, the plane
frail as a fly under the killer mountain?
Mural reflections, the outstretched Himalayas,

glittered on the swimming pool's surface
rising and falling gently, readying themselves
to vanish as I dived, in a dazzle of scribbles.

House of Snow

1. PAIN

No time to slow, stop,
look, to question leaf-twitch
or rustle, to lift up our eyes
to the hills. We must concentrate
our attention, keep moving
into the interior.

Even through boot-sole
rock and foot communicate,
a clash of cymbals. Feel
the ankle-stab, the long
thigh-front complaining strings,
joint-grind, jarring of vertebrae.

Earth and body converse as equals,
intimate as single combat.
Breathing and climbing are both
automatic and difficult. On this
irregular rock-ladder it is one step
one breath, heart and lungs struggling

tongue swollen with drought.
The mind has achieved
a dreamless freedom.
We stumble half asleep
inwards, upwards, into
less and less breathable air.

2. PUJA

We stand back gasping for breath while two late monks
urge on their ponies up the steep and broken track.
Maroon skirts flap in the dust-swirls.

In their embroidered chapel a noise like bees,
wordless to us; sometimes a cacophony
of horns, gongs, drums and air-shivering cymbals.

Walls and ceiling are gaudy with unknown stories.
Light winks from hanging satin cylinders,
shimmers in scarf-garlands of white and gold.

More and more butter-lamps are brought and clustered
below the giant bronze-faced Buddha
half smiling at all this opulence.

Ignorant but gripped, we sit shoeless against the wall
glad to be still at last, to look, to listen,
to breathe easily to the rhythm of the chant.

Outside, the prayer-wheel above its churning water
never rests, and flags strung out like washing
ripple unreadable words off in the wind.

3. STONE

They are breaking stones with sledgehammers' pock pock
and we pick our way off-balance through the heaps,
fresh surfaces surprisingly white with a slight shine.
New tourist lodges going up and those terrible
stairways of rock, not natural but made,
sheer-sided, viewing points for yet more rock,
the uninhabitable house of snow:
gables, roofs, towers appearing, disappearing,
spirit-teasing. Then swish! The curtain falls.

One morning we wake to find a skinned sky,
air icy-transparent, and unexpectedly
we walk among the great, as people imagined heaven:
Good morning, Socrates! Shakespeare – wonderful day!
We are all eyes and time is dead. Look now
westward, the snow is blinding, hard white,
needles and blades and massive tilted slabs.
But to the south the peaks are blue as dreams,
palest blue flowstone, solidifying sky.

This is your Life

Not mine, though. I am playing a bit-part
in someone else's, lucky extra
with a couple of scripted sentences
(not my own thoughts). I am Mrs Chips
the dear old schoolmistress. I haven't changed

she says. She has. It is only a dozen years
since she was the skinny, mousy one
on the left of the classroom, and now look:
blonde and tall as a daffodil with her fine
tanned skin, her athlete's slenderness.

Is she wondering *Is this all* (completed
at twenty-nine)? We sit in a fairy ring
in the hothouse studio, dressed in our best.
A handful of household names – some of her friends,
the popular presenter – are here made flesh

instead of coloured light. And I am touched
by celebrity's shine, wired up,
wined and partied, driven across London
behind dark glass through half-asleep streets,
past buildings palely lit, ghostly and magical.

Visiting My Daughter

She is sitting on the bed
in the corner of a room
that is a pale cube
of fluorescent light.

She has grown smaller
than twenty.
She could be a rag doll
among her stuffed animals.
A round face
emerges out of shapeless woolly clothes.
Small feet stick out
wearing children's socks.

The room smells faintly
of stale flowers, tangerines
and uneasy sleep.
A tall young doctor
crouches down to converse
on her level.
She speaks in a little dull voice –
and to the nurse, who interrogates her
from full height.
Yes, she has had her pills.
No, she doesn't want to go
and eat supper in the day room.

Once in a dream I turned
and saw her baby legs
in blue cablestitch tights
vanishing from a window.
I feel her falling now

not past the dirty glass
which to deter suicides
will scarcely open,
but through splinters of light
down through the hospital tower,
past foundations cracking open
into a deep place
crowded with shapes that she sees small but clearly.

I want to shriek, lunge,
grab at her, dig my nails in.
She wants to tell me
what it feels like to fall
and fall and fall
and what she sees
coming up to meet her.

Instead we make small talk
until it is time for my train –
I have a job to go to
fifty miles away.
I have to leave her huddled
in that high white corner.

Emma Knightley

I have lived all my life on a small lawn
like a piece of statuary: my job is to please.
I am young and beautiful (the true hazel eye)
and always tastefully dressed. I am the good daughter,
the good wife/sister/aunt and lady bountiful.
From time to time I have to behave
badly just to prove I exist. Not living up
to Mr Knightley's expectations is exhilarating,
though I suffer for it afterwards. The tears
are a second luxury.

I am not much of a reader but
I had an excellent governess.
In the long afternoons of needlework
or walks in the shrubbery while father
is lying down, I imagine being Rosalind
at large in the wild wood, or Viola
flung on a foreign shore,
striding out in trousers, defending myself:
my wits against the world.
In my Illyria, my magic isle
nothing would be surprising: that girl's
father might be a nobleman; that man
might cherish a secret passion; that woman
a broken heart. Busily I invent
delicate dramas for my acquaintances
but they disappoint me.

So here I am still in the same place
with a childish father,
a fatherly husband,
a handful of tedious neighbours.

Adored and pampered, I want for nothing.

Bathsheba Oak

It wasn't a matter of choice: which of three
was the best husband-material. There was
no debate, no adjudication. When I met Troy
the world shattered and reassembled around us:
in the dark a gleam of metal, a glossy eye,
a fiery strip of red. I breathed his breath.

If I shut my eyes I can see the leap of his sword,
an edge of light in an intricate dance.
He stood in a cage of glitter, laughing.
I thought: angels must look like this.

In spite of the coffin in the parlour, its faces
(mother and child) perfect as wax fruits in the candle-light,
in spite of his tears for her and his contempt for my
pleading, I wanted him back. After the absent years
I would have taken him back. He was heavy
at last in my arms and his pumping blood
was hot in my lap. Finally he belonged
only to me; my hands retraced his body, washing him.

I am grateful for Gabriel. He is a wall
to shield me from predators and the obsessions
of madmen. He is a feather bed, a fireside chair,
a loaf of bread. Predictable, an excellent
worker, very good with sheep. I lived my youth
in a short space and now we are Darby and Joan.
When he kisses me I keep my eyes open.

Sugarcraft

Too pretty to be true,
it is a day sculpted in sweetness.
Through firs iced in bright white
the level piste meanders
charmingly. Its violet grooves
entice the eye to bliss around the corner.

And here are the edible mannikins,
lords of all this Eden:
Alain, tall, slim and flexuous
in his école-de-ski strawberry uniform,
red-edged Bollé shades,
and me, smaller in complementary green
tilting my head to catch each honeyed
Gallic syllable from his lips.

And now his long feet in their yellow skis
dance over the glacé ground,
and he looks back laughing, calls to me
to lift my face up to the sun.
and every time we meet a little slope
I cry out in delightful fear.
Odd that a candied arm should bruise
with this black imprint of fingers.

Dialogue with Death

The website still shows him, live but motionless
in a series of snapshots: poised; leaping; falling;

landing on flowery grass in a silken shroud,
each of them with a backdrop of stone.

Again and again and again all day
he stood on top of the world. Feet found the edge,

sprang him up and out into emptiness
to hang for an instant like an angel of prey

so high above the hairsbreadth road, the tiny glinting river,
green strip of valley with its derisory habitations,

then plummet. Cold scoured his skin. Hair stood on end.
Don't pull the cord. Wait. Not yet not yet.

Then at the last moment the bone-shuddering jerk
as bursting parachute plucked him from his fall.

On the eighth occasion the valley has vanished.
He stands on his bright ledge breathing fast,

staring into blackness. The shadow
of his mountain cuts the opposite cliff.

Above: gold in the late sun under
fiery blue. Below: a slice of night.

He laughs as he jumps, asking himself how soon
eyes will adjust to loss of light.

Climber's Wife

He is a dark-faced stranger.
On the mountain, he says,
he thinks of me continually.
I loved his love of danger.

The bruising touch of rocks
has smudged his skin.
He thrums with tension,
gives off electric shocks.

In a glow of pain
our bodies thaw to life
but even then he is plotting
to be gone again.

We do not shut our eyes.
Behind his eyelids
lurks the deep green
of a fathomless crevasse.

My dreams are bright
with spindrift falling
and a thin body
headlong from white to white.

George Stubbs: The Milbanke and Melbourne Famil

The silken shine of money, that is the first thing
you notice about this group: the satin horse,
the lady's luminous cream and peach. And arrogance:
see how the right-hand man sits high
behind the fine arch of his horse's neck,
and the one in the middle, dandy in pastels,
lounges with decorous nonchalance. They are posing,
pleased with themselves. Look at their hands
in matte, pale, expensive gloves! Their spaniel
in the foreground crouches in adoration.

These must be relatives of Byron's Annabella,
that serious unsmiling girl, Lady Implacable –
though all that's in the future.
No hint of scandal smudges this clarity.

All the same, it was hubris, I think,
that made them choose that rugged cliff,
this stormcloud of a tree, for context. They think
nature is under their control. Wealth, servants,
unbending rectitude – all these
have perched then on creation's pinnacle.
But one limb of that oak, lumpy and wayward,
occupies half the picture,
overshadows them with its vigorous dark.
It will outlive the lot of them, horseflesh or human.

THE LONELYHEARTS COLUMN

1.

Like one of the circles of hell with the sexes
riding on contrary winds, men clockwise
and women widdershins, absorbed so deep
in their lonely concerns they don't even
wave to each other.

There are no mirrors here, obsessed
with appearances they squint the mind's eye
to see themselves forever young,
well-preserved, youthful, 55 going on 20,
but underneath is fear.

Middle-aged rich men dream of childwomen
half their age to cherish:
Knight, 49, seeks young attractive damsel
to rescue from distress. His desperation
pursues her as his grail.

The women think of endings rather than beginning
again. There are too many *young-looking widows,*
fiftysomething blonde divorcees, early-retired ageless ladies.
They know that makebelieve must terminate,
long to be settled before darkness falls.

2.

Stylish romantic
Every morning Narcissus
early 40s
very successful financially
admires his reflection
tall, dark, handsome
and makes his wish.
WLTM
beautiful blonde counterpart
The magic mirror answers:
Lonely and lustful
in vain are you vain.
Money is trash
and time is passing.

Ladies, don't look at the small man
between the lines!

3.

professional widower
fit, slim, successful

The professional widower
bides his time
spinning bright webs
in the darkness of his skull.

WLTM attractive solvent lady
for exclusive relationship

He has serially set up
several homes
with several partners
all pretty, all affluent.

without emotional baggage
children or pets

Househunting, he takes a particular interest
in bathrooms. The ensuite facilities
attached to the master bedroom
must be alluring, with room for manoeuvre,
secluded, without a window.

A man of regular habits.
The neighbours notice him
departing each morning
blowing a kiss as he closes
the glossy front door.

Then, one evening, the outcry!
The ringing, the knocking,
the trembling hands,
staring eyes, stammered horror!

ideally her relatives are dead

4.

musician seeks lady for inspiration
struggling novelist seeks lady of means

Are these invocations to muses, and do the Olympians
look through the lonelyhearts columns?
Is that where Zeus found those languishing ladies
Danae and Leda to practise deceptions on?

Here men have posted their small prayers to the daughters
of Zeus. Come to me, Euterpe, patroness of the flute,
Terpsichore, make the blood dance in my veins.
Polyhymnia, kindle my sacred flame.

The writer in his garret will not wish to entertain
Calliope, goddess of long poems. Would he welcome tragedy queen
Melpomene, or find giggly Thalia more fun?
Perhaps he seeks not muse but sugar-mammy
to sweeten his toils with kisses and chocolate.

5.

He knows what she looks like,
would recognise her anywhere
instantly, has built her himself
feature by feature.
In tedious meetings
or the crowded tube
raptness betrays him. Shut
in the studio of his skull
he is chipping away, smoothing ,
appraising. His lips tighten.
She is blonde,
5'6", 130lbs, attractive,
nice figure, about 30.
She undulates, all curves.
He loves the spring of hair
from her forehead, the firm rise
and decline of breast and buttock,
spoons of hollow below her neck
so intimately known.
But what of the soul
not formable by tool or hand?
He assumes that gratitude
will show itself in panting
eagerness to please, and hopes
against the odds for warmth
in what he has conjured
from dream-film or from stone.

6.

lone sailor seeks first mate

The lone sailor
stands at the wheel
his hair enlivened
by the salty breeze.
His blue eyes scan
the sky for weather,
the horizon for landfall.

Alas, I am a feeble
voyager, the trip
to Eddystone Lighthouse
a childhood ordeal,
the youthful crossing
from Brindisi to Piraeus
a rite of suffering.

They say life is a journey.
I caught my sailor
but after thirteen hours
in a cramped bunk
swung up and down and sideways
in a force five wind
and a rolling swell

never was land more fervently
blessed by pope or king
than shining Cherbourg.
So I threw back my sailor
who shortly after married
a lady with a boat
and a strong stomach.

7.

Pierced lad with great physique
seeks stilettoed lady with good legs

The late light gleams on
St. Sebastian's
fine musculature
highlighted with sweat,
on bright arrow-shafts
and runnels of blood
from myriad punctures.

Transfixed, as his gaze
dims he can only
yearn across space at
the knife-thrower's girl,
her eyes glazed with fear
and her star-flung limbs
outlined in chill steel.

8.

You'd think they were buying a pot
or picture, or had set their hearts
eccentrically on something awkward and English
like an Aga, to grace their foreign houses.

I was briefly tempted by the sheep-farmer
in the Dordogne, though too old, too plain
for the adventurous American or the landowner
on the Costa del Sol seeking a warm soul.

Well, I am the wrong kind of woman,
too settled, too much at home
in this particular damp valley,
held here like Frost's silken tent.

But how can one man presume
to be a stranger's world
or like a felled branch in a river
acquiesce in any sad flotsam.

9.

Pyknic is how Doreen described us.
Dumpy was my husband's epithet.
Like daughter, mother, grandmothers, I am
not narrow. Chubby child, tubby teenager.

You are definitely slim
says the young 38 businessman.
Are you slim? asks the professional
early 40s male. *You – slender, attractive,*
states the Midlands-based man
with varied interests.
Are meagre women more intelligent then?
More loyal, more loving, better in bed?
You can hurt yourself on a thin woman,
according to Richard.

But look, this romantic architect
seeks fun-loving girl, any build,
 and here, hurrah, a French gentleman
wishes to meet a *very buxom lady*
- alas, much younger than me.

10.

GSOH

O let my love be a light woman
who will kick up her heels and scamper
over the quaking ground, a small ray
of sunshine to drive dull care away.

We'll banish the lacrymae rerum
from our gaudy night, our jamboree,
our mardi gras. We'll paint the town red,
live in a cherry bowl, a rosy bed.

The thin crust of love is undermined
by caves where blind white creatures scuttle,
but let us eat, drink and be merry,
hoot, chuckle and chortle, split our sides
and fall about. We shall die laughing
at last, we shall kill ourselves laughing.

LEARNING TO LOOK

ART CLASS 1

We are not looking at the daisies
but at the darkness behind them
that pushes in among their petals.
It is not the colour of darkness
that matters, but its shape.

Today I have learnt the difference
between water-colour: weak
and gouache: strong. The spiky
arrowhead spaces between
my daisy petals are strong. Violent.

Like a driver in a fast car
I have a sense of power behind my brush.
I fill it with midnight and draw
on my empty paper
darkness, threatening with edges.

Then I can see
what is left after the inky black-blue
has been recorded:
white jagged blanks,
the alienness of flowers.

ART CLASS 2

The blackened ones are brutal,
medieval weapons – mace and morningstar –
skullsplitters in miniature,

a far cry from children's toys.
I carefully arrange my five
conker cases (intact ones for beginners).

First a line drawing
looking at shapes and spaces
then a portrait of shadows.

Today we are learning the difference
between shade and blackness,
lack of light and death of colour.

The tutor is drawing concave
and convex with a soft pencil.
Her conker shell is split:

one half a cup of twilight
and in the other, the fruit
swelling with fiery shine,

a precious thing precisely fitted,
spotlit from the left. And her
left ear, too, is beautiful.

From where I stand behind,
it is an ear of flame.

I know the feel of roundness. I remember
my baby's weight on my arm, all parts
of him hemispherical: forehead,
cheek and downy crown, belly and buttock.

This is the season of globes, and of the brief
beauty of conkers. I have drawn the not-circular
outline, the fingerprint on top a swirl
of lighter stripes edging the centre,

and now I am making it solid with rings of shading
around the bulges, denser and denser shadows.
Grey is the wrong colour. In a fine fog
of smudge the object seems to dent the page

like a nut-shaped nugget of ore from the limestone below us.
But this is alive. Its neat markings will dull
and swell with the shoot which aspires to be
a tree of candles in the upper air.

ART CLASS 4

We sank down from the dazzle
of white peaks into the shades of grey
cloud and pollution – the real world
with its small mountains
its city streets and smells.

I was washing my palette
during the sharing-out of colours
so the spectrum was all allotted.
What was left for me
were shades of grey.

And I was away
airborne, when the collage
was pieced together,
so it must have lacked
my vital undertones.

Grey was ' the new black'
that season, and silver
the in thing for accessories, so fashion
pages provided a wealth
of muted tones, though curiously

what I had seized on
and stashed away as grey
emerged into other lights as blue,
brown, green, a whole
gamut of glaucousness.

Diversity of texture
as well as shade: my greys
were fur, feather and lace, the burnished curves
of steel, patterns of tree
and tendril. Live greys

not lacking, moribund and dry
but drab with the unpretentiousness
of seeds whose small bulk
is crammed to bursting
with the impatient future.

Bright smoke, Romeo's oxymoron,
realised at Ribblehead – the stagnant
fog of all that morning suffused
suddenly, radiant haze – and I drove
home into clarity. My low-browed
house a lantern full of light.

As we consider the connotations of December
the fog is catching up with Askrigg,
now down with a numbing weight and silence,
now flying uphill. In, out, in, out
I flicker through shifting time-zones
and continents, roles and responsibilities.

Christmas, a time of feasting and heartache
when families, scattered like ashes, struggle
to reassemble. Jan's children
know there is no money for Christmas presents;
my mother feels unequal to the customary
baking my father cannot eat this year.

We are creating Christmas cards. Mine seems banal,
trivial. I lack skill in drawing and patience to learn
watercolouring, which alone could capture
these sad-beautiful sliding scarves of bright
and dark, redesigning moment by moment
our loveliest of landscapes and the sky.

ART CLASS 6

Perspective, our New Year study,
starts with dead wood, last autumn's
prunings turned to objets d'art
espaliered on coloured rectangles.
Seen from the side they lean into the room
three-dimensional, in a mime of eagerness.

Novices opposite perceive them flat,
irregular black lattice. And that is hard
enough to draw. Branch-crossings fuse
to joints and junctions through my reading glasses.
Strong lenses see subtler relationships
but cannot keep the page in focus.

As we grow older our precious eyes
themselves distort shape and colour.
My mother's retina bends uprights, interposes
a grey round cloud, and Judith's
when she moves, a rain of ash. My eyelids
are loose shutters giving and stealing.

Shapes are netted among the branches:
here is a square inside a triangle,
a crooked diamond, snippets of circles.
Two shoots rise straight and parallel,
then lean together as if a rectangle
longed to be gothic arch.

My neighbour disregards the crude background
panels of colour, paints her interstices
in crazy pavings of red, pink, orange, yellow
as if the twigs are incidental
as lead-seams in a stained-glass window,
or stone walls on the hill behind our classroom.

ART CLASS 7

How do you look at a cube?
Only the mind's eye sees equality,
angles of ninety degrees in three
planes, six sides uniformly
white, twelve crisp edges.

Today our eyes are assailed
by whitewashed boxes on boxes
beside and behind boxes
all facing the same way.
. From southeast I look at corners:

at eye-level, flat; higher up,
shallow peaks; below, angular valleys
revealing lid. Baffled, I draw
what I think I ought to see, and my scale
is out, my boxes swell to buildings,

sheer sunblanched city (silent,
bare, like Wordsworth's London)
pinklit from the side with promise
of perfect day. But in each box
of breath what griefs are surfacing?

Double vision should be twice as good
but which eye to believe?
Trust neither mouth
of a two-headed speaker.

Artfully draped, this cloth
reduplicates its swerving stripes
to frenzy. Blue, blue-green,
green-grey, whitish, over and over.

It is a winter landscape
of pleated hills, bare woods,
ravines, slung valleys.
Here the north-facing slope

falls duck-egg blue with frost.
Up there, a swathe
of faded bents, a strip of olive
meadow. Indigo distances.

My right eye, dazzled by low sun,
sees everything blue. Above the river
floats a sapphire stream. Each piece
of gravel on the track is twinned with turquoise.

It's not so much learning to look as re-learning.
The child took so long to walk home to lunch
there wasn't time to eat. I only remember
the fascination of earthworms and roadworks.
Now, my weekly journey to Askrigg is magical.
The car protects me from too much seeing

or I might never arrive. The high point comes
after the tortuous climb past Crow Trees
and the slow threading through icepuddles
and greened-over spoil-heaps, in a shock of emptiness
when the whole of Upper Wensleydale opens
under its miles of air. Glimmer of Semerwater
in its hollow. Addlebrough rising slowly
from the brownness as I descend.

Since I began coming it has been mostly
winter, colours damped down. Grey-brown of rock
and heather. Buff and khaki winter grass.
Sometimes a thin snow has repainted
the long ridges in cloud colours. At last
I know how to use my collection of greys.

They range from almost black to off-white
via pinkish, mushroom-beige, greenish,
dull-blue – drabness rich in potential.
Blue at the top, green at the bottom, charcoal
and brown for hills. My shades of grey make up
the colours of wilderness, this grave place
beautiful even in rain, vital,
not needing the sun to shine.

The Sunday supplement cover girl
is unaware of the camera.
Under her shaggy hair her dark eyebrows
frown at a flower, interrogating. Is this
Flower? Can this be
Red?
She knows the flimsiness
of petals, skinsmooth to the finger,
their sharp or heavysweet,
vanilla or peppery scent,
but not this precision of shape,
assault of colour.
For her, this is the first flower.
It stops her in her tracks.

I have three tubes of red
and others to alter them. I should like
to paint this miniature rose
but how could my brush follow the edges of petals,
their unexpected swoops and points, their thinness,
rimmed (this one) by a hairsbreadth of light?
How paint the degrees of concavity, the just-opening
overlapping sections of globe at the centre?
The convex, occasionally curling-under
outer petals? The shadows made by lamp
and window? Reflections, translucencies,
in every red from vermilion to magenta?
And the slight veininess like minuscule
wave-patterns in sand?

I put my paints away.
I have seen it now.
I think I shall remember.